# Pop Bottle SCIENCE

by Lynn Brunelle

with illustrations by Paul Meisel

**Workman Publishing, New York**

**For my brother, Bill, who was my first guide to seeing the sizzle-boom-bang-pop in things**

### Acknowledgments

I would like to thank all the official testers who helped me put together the experiments in this book. I couldn't have done it without Jacob, Alfie, and Jess. And I would like to thank Keith, Kai, Jon, Tracy, Bill, Mom and Dad, Toshi, and Mary for emptying out so many pop bottles in the name of science.

Workman books are available at special discounts when purchased in bulk for premiums and sales promotions as well as for fund-raising or educational use. Special editions or book excerpts can also be created to specification. For details, contact the Special Sales Director at the address below, or send an email to specialmarkets@workman.com.

Workman Publishing Company, Inc.
225 Varick Street
New York, NY 10014-4381
workman.com

WORKMAN is a registered trademark
of Workman Publishing Co., Inc.

Printed in China
ISBN 978-0-7611-2980-6
29 28 27 26

# Contents

## Mysterious Molecules · 1

## Pushes and Pulls · 13

# Blasts, Bangs, Twists, and Other Reactions · 47

# Secrets of Earth and Space · 67

# Bottled Weather · 79

# Plants and Other Living Things · 91

# Light, Sight, Hearing, and Breathing · 109

# Welcome to Pop Bottle Science!

**M**eet your Pop Bottle. It's a perfect miniature science lab. You can see through it, and it holds things. Your Pop Bottle also has a special feature other bottles don't have: a removable, funnel-shaped top.

Some of the experiments and projects in this book require using the whole Pop Bottle. Others use only parts of the Pop Bottle. Still others ask you to use *another* bottle. (Often this is because your Pop Bottle is not watertight.)

 *This icon means another bottle (plastic only) should be used.*

 *This icon means you should ask an adult to help you. Many of the experiments and projects could make a mess if you're not careful.*

Experimentation and exploration have been characteristics of mankind since the dawn of time. Building knowledge through curiosity defines the human species.

*Pop Bottle Science* is just the tip of the iceberg. Keep your eyes and mind open and never stop asking questions. Maybe with something as simple as a pop bottle, you'll be on your way to finding the answers.

## Science projects are lots of fun, but they do require care.

- Read and follow instructions. If an experiment doesn't work, chances are that you skipped a step or some crucial element. Go back and try again.

- Never use matches, heat, sharp objects, or poisonous substances without an adult to help you.

- If you're unsure about doing a project in the house, ask your mom or dad for permission.

- Don't make substitutions; use only the materials listed. The experiment may not work or, worse, you could hurt yourself by using other materials.

- Remember that movies are make-believe! Don't fool around with liquid mixtures. Never drink one.

## You'll have much more fun if you do these experiments and projects with care!

# **Mysterious Molecules**

## move it!

### do water molecules move or stay still?

### **WHAT DO YOU NEED?**
- *Your Pop Bottle with the top part removed*
- *Water*
- *Food coloring*

### **WHAT DO YOU DO?**

*1.* Fill your Pop Bottle about three-quarters full with water.

*2.* Add 6 or 7 drops of food coloring into your bottle of water. Notice how the coloring falls to the bottom, leaving a trail.

**3.** Don't touch the bottle. Leave it alone for a few hours.

**4.** Check on your bottle. What does the water look like?

## WHAT'S GOING ON?

**W**ater molecules are always moving. The molecules bounce and bump against each other until the color is evenly dispersed throughout the water in the bottle.

The process by which molecules exchange places is called *diffusion,* a phenomenon that occurs in all states of matter: liquids, solids, and gases. Diffusion in the air, for instance, causes the fragrance of flowers to spread all around a room.

# ┃aper magic
## can papeR stay dRy in wateR?

## WHAT DO YOU NEED?
- *Wadded-up paper*
- *Your Pop Bottle with the top part removed*
- *A bucket or large bowl filled halfway with water*

### WHAT DO YOU DO?

*1.* Stuff the paper into the bottom of your Pop Bottle. Check to be sure the paper stays in the bottom and won't fall out when you turn the bottle upside down.

*2.* Turn your Pop Bottle upside down, and push it straight down into the bucket of water. (Be sure the bottle is vertical, and don't tilt the bottle!)

*3.* Lift your Pop Bottle out of the water. (Again, be sure not to tilt the bottle.)

*4.* Remove the dry paper.

### WHAT'S GOING ON?

The paper in the bottle was protected by air. As you pushed the bottle down, the air pushed down on the water. This prevented the bottle from filling with water, and the paper stayed dry.

# lava lamp

## why doesn't oil mix with water?

### WHAT DO YOU NEED?

- A pop bottle (Make sure the cap is screwed on tight!)
- Vegetable oil
- Food coloring
- Water

## WHAT DO YOU DO?

*1.* Fill the bottle about one-third of the way with vegetable oil.

*2.* Add a couple drops of food coloring.

*3.* Carefully fill up the bottle with water. (This should be done over the sink, in case some water spills over.)

*4.* Tighten the cap. Let the bottle sit, allowing the oil and water to fully separate.

*5.* Slowly rock the bottle back and forth and watch the wave.

## WHAT'S GOING ON?

**W**ater is heavier than oil. This makes water stay on the bottom of the bottle, while the oil oozes to the top.

# add it up

## does one plus one always equal two?

## WHAT DO YOU NEED?

- *Masking tape*
- *Your Pop Bottle with the top part removed*
- *Water*

- *Rubbing alcohol (Caution: Alcohol is poisonous and should be used only with a grown-up present)*
- *A ruler*

## WHAT DO YOU DO?

*1.* Place 2 pieces of masking tape vertically on the outside of your Pop Bottle.

*2.* Measure 2 cups of water, and pour them into your bottle.

*3.* Mark the water level on one piece of tape, and write the number *1*.

*4.* Dump out the water.

*5.* Pour 1 cup of water into the bottle.

*6.* Pour 1 cup of rubbing alcohol into the bottle.

*7.* Mark the new level on the second tape, and write the number *2*.

*8.* Measure level 1 and level 2 and compare the result. The second level should be the same as the first level—but is it?

## WHAT'S GOING ON?

**W**ater has lots of empty spaces between its molecules. Alcohol molecules are strung closer to each other. When the two combine, the alcohol molecules fall into the spaces in between the water molecules. The alcohol molecules slip like loose sand into the cracks between rocks.

# water riddle

## can you make water grow?

### WHAT DO YOU NEED?

- *A plastic pop bottle you can mark up (Don't do this experiment with a glass bottle.)*
- *Water*
- *A marker*
- *A freezer*

### WHAT DO YOU DO?

*1.* Fill the bottle three-quarters full with tap water and cap it.

*2.* Make a mark to show where the water level is.

*3.* Place the bottle upright in the freezer. Be sure that no water is leaking out.

*4.* Check the water level the next day.

### WHAT'S GOING ON?

There are three common states of matter on Earth: liquids, gases, and solids. Matter undergoes a molecular change when it passes from one state to another. This change is in the density of its molecules, and temperature can make change happen. You made water "grow" by changing the density of its molecules when it froze.

# into thin air

inflate
a balloon
with science.

## WHAT DO YOU NEED?

- *Balloon*
- *A plastic pop bottle*
- *Water*
- *Two saucepans*

## WHAT DO YOU DO?

*1.* Fit a balloon over the bottle's mouth.

*2.* Fill a saucepan with hot tap water.

*3.* Fill the second saucepan with cold water.

*4.* Place the bottle in the hot water saucepan. Watch what happens.

*5.* Remove the bottle from the hot water and put it in the cold water. What happens?

## WHAT'S GOING ON?

**H**eat gives air molecules energy, and that energy makes them move faster. As the molecules spread out, they took up more room and filled the balloon. Cold makes air molecules slow down. The molecules lost energy, settled down, and become more densely packed in the bottle. As this happened, the balloon sagged.

# burping bottle

## can you make a bottle burp?

### WHAT DO YOU NEED?

- A sturdy, 1-liter plastic bottle
- A freezer
- Water
- A quarter

### WHAT DO YOU DO?

*1.* Put the empty, uncapped bottle in the freezer for an hour (or longer).

*2.* Run some tap water over a quarter, and get it wet.

*3.* After an hour is up, pull the bottle out and immediately put the wet quarter on the mouth of the bottle, covering the whole opening.

*4.* Set the bottle on the counter, wait, and watch.

### WHAT'S GOING ON?

Cold air is denser than warm air: cold air molecules move more slowly and take up less space. Inside the freezer, the air became compressed, and this made room for more cool air molecules to flow into the bottle.

When you took the bottle out of the freezer, the cool air molecules warmed up to room temperature. The wet quarter created a seal on the bottle opening so that the air inside, still densely packed, couldn't escape. The bottle was not too crowded with air molecules in the freezer, but, at room temperature, the molecules began moving faster and taking up more and more space. The pressure built inside the bottle until some air had to escape. So it did—through the mouth of the bottle. The pressure was strong enough to move the coin as the air burped past it.

# water and ice
## Why does ice Float?

### WHAT DO YOU NEED?
- *Your Pop Bottle with the top part removed*
- *Cooking oil*
- *An ice cube*

### WHAT DO YOU DO?

*1.* Fill the bottle about half full with the cooking oil.

*2.* Drop the ice cube in, and watch what happens as the cube melts.

### WHAT'S GOING ON?

An ice cube looks more solid than oil, but its molecules are a lot less densely packed together. When the ice melts and turns to liquid water, the molecules become denser. You can see that happen when the melted drops fall in perfect little spheres down through the oil, coming to rest at the bottom of the bottle.

# color show

## diffeRences in density make Liquid FiRewoRks.

### WHAT DO YOU NEED?

- A tablespoon
- Cooking oil
- A jar with a lid
- Food coloring in a few different colors
- Your Pop Bottle with the top part removed
- Water

### WHAT DO YOU DO?

*1.* Measure 1 tablespoon of oil into the jar.

*2.* Drop different food colorings into the jar (2 or 3 drops of each color).

*3.* Put the cover on the jar, and shake it up.

*4.* Fill your Pop Bottle almost full of tap water.

*5.* Pour your oil color mixture on top, using the inverted top of the bottle as a funnel, and watch the color show.

## WHAT'S GOING ON?

**W**ater is denser than oil. If the two are mixed together, they will always separate. Food coloring is mostly water so the drops of coloring sink through the oil and down to the water level. When the bubbles sink, their oil coating rises back to the surface. The tiny color drops just seem to disappear because each tiny drop of coloring isn't strong enough to change the color of the water. Over time all the tiny drops will sink and the water color will change.

# quicksand
## Liquid OR SOLid?

## WHAT DO YOU NEED?
- *Water*
- *Food coloring*
- *Cornstarch*
- *Your Pop Bottle (with the top removed)*

## WHAT DO YOU DO?

*1.* Measure ½ cup of water.

*2.* Add food coloring to the water.

*3.* Pour ½ pound of cornstarch into your Pop Bottle.

*4.* Slowly add the dyed water to the cornstarch and stir the mixture carefully.

*5.* Once all the starch has been mixed, conduct some tests. Stir the quicksand.

The faster you stir, the harder the quicksand becomes. The slower you stir, the runnier the quicksand gets. Let it run through your fingers. Then give your quicksand a squeeze.

*6.* Is it a solid or a liquid?

## WHAT'S GOING ON?

Quicksand may sometimes act like a solid, but it doesn't keep a regular shape, so it's a liquid. Your "quicksand" is a special kind of liquid that becomes thicker, rather than thinner, when stirred.

**NOTE**: Don't pour your quicksand down the drain! It willl clog the pipes.

# Pushes and Pulls

## card trick

can you turn a bottle full of water upside down and not spill a drop?

### WHAT DO YOU NEED?

- A sturdy, 1-liter plastic bottle
- Water
- Sink
- A playing card

## WHAT DO YOU DO?

*1.* Fill the bottle up to the very top with tap water. The water should come right to the edge of the mouth of the bottle.

*2.* Hold the bottle over a sink and place the playing card over the top of the mouth of the bottle. Hold the card in place firmly and turn the bottle upside down.

*3.* Carefully remove your hand, leaving the playing card in place. (Don't jiggle the card!)

*4.* The card stays put and the water stays inside the bottle even though it's upside down!

## WHAT'S GOING ON?

If you just turned a bottle of water upside down, the water would come out because it's pulled down by gravity. But another force, air pressure, is pushing up on the card. It creates a seal, and that seal is more powerful than the force of gravity. But watch it! If you bump the card, the water will come pouring out.

# gravity's air force

## can you poke a hole in a bottle and not spring a leak?

### WHAT DO YOU NEED?

- *A plastic pop bottle with a cap*
- *Water*
- *A hammer and nail—and a grown-up to help you*
- *A sink*

### WHAT DO YOU DO?

*1.* Fill your bottle right to the rim with water, and tighten the cap.

*2.* About three-quarters of the way down the bottle, poke a hole by gently hammering a nail through the plastic.

*3.* Nothing comes out of the hole!

*4.* Now hold the bottle over the sink, and loosen the cap. What happens now?

### WHAT'S GOING ON?

**Y**ou just showed something very important about air. It is a major enforcer of the law of gravity. Without air pushing down on it, the water stayed put. But when you loosened the cap, air rushed in and pushed the water out.

You also showed something important about water. Molecules on the surface of water cling together and form a kind of "skin." This is known as *surface tension.*

### FIND OUT MORE

**N**ow that you have a bottle with a hole in it, try the **Super Squirter!** (page 30).

# ride the water

## Why can bugs walk on the surface of water?

### WHAT DO YOU NEED?

- *Your Pop Bottle (with the top removed)*
- *Water*
- *Black pepper instead of bugs (Large grains work best)*

### WHAT DO YOU DO?

*1.* Fill your Pop Bottle with water.

**2.** Lightly sprinkle black pepper on the surface of the water. What does the pepper do?

## WHAT'S GOING ON?

If you look at the water just right, you'll see small dimples around the pepper grains. This is because the pepper isn't actually floating. It is riding on the water's surface the way you could ride on top of a huge air balloon.

Water's surface tension, like the skin of a balloon, can be strong enough to hold things if the objects are the right size and weight. What makes surface tension so strong?

Water's clinging power is strongest on the surface because nothing is pulling the water molecules upward. In fact, the surface is pressed downward by air pressure. Also, water molecules on the surface cling only to neighbor molecules on the sides and below.

Other water molecules, deeper in the water, have molecules tugging at them from all directions. These factors make water's surface a very interesting place.

# magic finger

## can you make pepper run away from your finger?

### WHAT DO YOU NEED?

- *Your Pop Bottle (with the top removed)*
- *Water*
- *Black pepper*
- *A bar of soap*

### WHAT DO YOU DO?

*1.* Fill your Pop Bottle with water.

*2.* Sprinkle black pepper on the water's surface.

*3.* Touch the middle of the water on the surface with your fingertip. Nothing will happen (other than a wet fingertip).

*4.* Now rub your fingertip on the bar of soap.

*5.* Touch the middle of the water on the surface with your soapy fingertip. What happens to the pepper now?

## WHAT'S GOING ON?

**I**t may seem that the pepper was changed by the soap, but actually the soap changed the water's surface tension.

Soap molecules have the power to mix with water molecules and make water molecules less clingy with one another. (This is what soap does to dirt and stains, too.) As the water molecules relaxed their tight grip on one another, the surface relaxed and pushed outward. In this experiment, the pepper rode to the sides of the bottle along with the soap, away from your finger.

# scooting paper

## can you make a paper fish swim?

## WHAT DO YOU NEED?

- *Paper*
- *Your Pop Bottle (with the top removed)*
- *Water*
- *Detergent (vegetable oil works too)*

## WHAT DO YOU DO?

*1.* Draw a fish on a piece of paper. Cut out the shape. Next, cut a thin channel from the tail to the middle of the body. Make a round hole, as shown.

*2.* Fill your Pop Bottle about halfway with water.

*3.* Carefully place the paper fish on the water.

*4.* Add a drop of detergent into the hole. Watch what happens!

## WHAT'S GOING ON?

**T**he drop of detergent changed the water's surface tension. The fish was propelled because it was in contact with two different surface tensions: one with the detergent and one with plain water.

# pop bottle cap drops

## how many drops of water can you fit on the top of a bottle cap?

## WHAT DO YOU NEED?

- ■ *Two pop bottle tops*
- ■ *Water dropper*
- ■ *Water*
- ■ *Dishwashing detergent*

## WHAT DO YOU DO?

*1.* Take two dry pop bottle caps and place them flat side up on a counter.

*2.* Fill your water dropper.

*3.* Drip a drop of water on the cap.

*4.* How many drops of water can you fit on this first cap?

*5.* Now put a single drop of liquid detergent on the other cap. Then wipe the detergent off.

*6.* How many drops of water can you fit on this second cap?

## WHAT'S GOING ON?

As you dripped drops on the first cap, the drops of water stuck together due to the natural cohesion of water molecules. You could keep adding drops until there was too much water and the surface tension was broken.

The film of detergent on the second cap makes it harder for drops of water to form in a group. Fewer drops can be added because soap prevents water molecules from joining together and forming surface tension.

# bubble maker

## why are bubbles always round?

### WHAT DO YOU NEED?

- *A bowl*
- *Water*
- *Liquid dishwashing soap*
- *Sugar*
- *The top of your Pop Bottle (without the rest of the bottle and without the cap)*
- *A space outdoors*

### WHAT DO YOU DO?

*1.* Fill a bowl halfway with water.

*2.* Add several squirts of dishwashing detergent and a teaspoon of sugar. (Based on the size of the bowl you're using, experiment with different amounts of each.)

*3.* Stir the mixture in the bowl until it's mixed and bubbly.

*4.* Take the bowl and the top of your bottle outside.

*5.* Dip the mouth of the bottle into the mixture. Lift it up and blow through the hole. You should get some pretty terrific bubbles. (Try blowing through both openings—the bottle mouth and the wider opening as well. See if the bubbles change.)

## WHAT'S GOING ON?

**A** bubble is a drop of water with air in the middle. Air inside the bubble pushes outward in all directions against the watery skin. At the same time, the watery skin is pushing inward against the air. Water molecules are attracted to each other, and if water had its way, the bubble would collapse into a water drop. These equal forces of pushing out, and pushing in, create a shape with boundaries at an equal distance from the center. This shape is a sphere—the only shape a bubble can be.

# weighty water

which hole in a bottle will squirt the farthest?

## WHAT DO YOU NEED?

- *A plastic pop bottle with cap*
- *Water*
- *A hammer and nail and an adult to help you poke holes*
- *Sink (or outside area that's okay to get wet)*

## WHAT DO YOU DO?

*1.* Fill up the pop bottle with water and cap it tightly.

*2.* Get a grown-up to help you hammer four holes in a vertical row starting about 1 inch from the bottom. They must all be the same size and spaced about 1 inch apart, going straight up. As long as the cap is on tight, water won't squirt out the holes.

*3.* Hold your bottle anyplace where it's okay to spring a leak (like a sink), and uncap it.

## WHAT'S GOING ON?

**I**magine that each hole in your bottle represents a layer of water. The bottom layer supports the weight of all the layers above it. This creates pressure at the bottom, and that is why the lower holes shoot the farthest. The hole near the top squirts the least because there is less water weight at the top and less pressure.

Water reacts strongly to gravity, and a small difference in height can make a big difference in water weight. If you dive to the bottom of the pool, you can feel the water pushing down on you. The deeper you go, the more water is pushing down above you, and the more squashed you feel.

# drop it

## WiLL a FULL boTTLe FaLL TWice as FasT as a haLF-FULL boTTLe?

**WHAT DO YOU NEED?**

- *A friend to watch your experiment*
- *Two pop bottles of the same size*
- *Water*
- *A safe, high place to drop the bottles from—you can stand on a chair*

GO!

**WHAT DO YOU DO?**

*1.* Fill one bottle up to the top with water and put the cap on.

*2.* Fill the other bottle halfway and cap it.

*3.* Make a prediction: Which bottle will hit the ground first?

*4.* Take both bottles and hold them equally high off the ground. Position your pal so that he or she can see the bottles hit the ground.

**5.** Drop both bottles at the same time, being careful not to hit your friend.

**6.** Which bottle hits first?

**7.** Experiment with different amounts of water. Does it make any difference?

## WHAT'S GOING ON?

**A**n object's weight has no effect on how fast it falls. The speed of a fall may be affected by an object's shape, due to surface area. That's why a pin falls faster than a feather. But your two bottles have the same surface area and should hit the ground at the same time. The bottles should hit the ground at the same time. Galileo—a great scientist from the seventeenth century— discovered that no matter how much an object weighs, it should fall at the same rate. Ask any grown-up to guess which bottle will fall faster. Does anyone get it right?

# squirt bottle battle

*may the best squirter win!*

## WHAT DO YOU NEED?

- *Several plastic pop bottles—try different sizes, but make sure each bottle has a tight-fitting cap*
- *Different-sized nails and a hammer, a drill, thumbtacks— anything that will make large and small holes (along with an adult to help you)*
- *Water*
- *A battleground and some buddies ready to get soaked*

## WHAT DO YOU DO?

*1.* Make a variety of different holes in your pop bottle caps. Use several caps and experiment with different-sized holes for each one.

*2.* Fill up your pop bottles with water and put the caps on tightly.

*3.* Stand back and squirt! Which cap sprays the farthest? Which pop bottle squirter has the biggest stream?

## WHAT'S GOING ON?

**T**he size of the hole determines how big the stream will be and how far you can squirt. A smaller hole creates a smaller and longer stream. A larger hole creates a bigger and shorter stream. The reason for the difference is the amount of pressure acting on the water.

When you squeeze the bottle, you put pressure on the water inside. The water inside wants to get outside quickly. If there's a small hole, more pressure is created because it's crowded at the exit hole. More pressure means more energy and more energy means the water is pushed harder, and a longer distance is achieved. The stream may be a tiny one, but it can really travel.

With a larger hole, more water can get out at the same time, so the stream is wider. But because there is less pressure, the stream has less energy and travels a shorter distance.

# inside-out balloon

can you turn a balloon inside out using air pressure?

## WHAT DO YOU NEED?

- *A nail and a hammer to make holes (and an adult to help you)*
- *A plastic pop bottle, the bigger the better*
- *A balloon*

## WHAT DO YOU DO?

*1.* Get an adult to help you make a nail hole near the bottom of the bottle.

*2.* Dangle a balloon inside the bottle. Stretch the mouth of the balloon over the mouth of the bottle, and blow up the balloon as much as you possibly can, so that it inflates within the pop bottle.

*3.* Put a finger over the nail hole that was made near the bottom of the bottle.

*4.* Take your mouth away from the top of the balloon.

*5.* Take your finger off the hole.

## WHAT'S GOING ON?

**T**he air in the bottle was pushed out the nail hole when you inflated the balloon. When you removed your thumb, air rushed back into the bottle. At the same time, air rushed out of the balloon. The combination of forces was strong enough to turn the balloon inside out.

# super squirter!

design your own super-squirter water cannon.

## WHAT DO YOU NEED?

- *A nail and a hammer, to make holes (and an adult to help you)*
- *A plastic pop bottle, the bigger the better*
- *A balloon*
- *Water*
- *Someone to soak*

## WHAT DO YOU DO?

*1.* Get an adult to help you make a nail hole near the bottom of the bottle.

*2.* Make a nail hole in a bottle cap and put the cap aside for now.

*3.* Dangle a balloon inside the bottle. Stretch

the mouth of the balloon over the mouth of the bottle. Fill the balloon with water.

**4.** While the water is still flowing, and when the balloon is full, put your thumb over the nail hole.

**5.** Turn off the water.

**6.** Carefully place the cap on the bottle and tighten it. (Don't take your thumb off the hole!)

**7.** Go to a place that's okay to get wet.

**8.** Ready? Aim! Take your thumb off the hole!

### WHAT'S GOING ON?

**W**hen the nail hole is plugged, the pop bottle protects the balloon from being acted on by air pressure. But when you take your thumb off the hole, that persistent air pressure pushes hard into the hole. The air pushes on the rubbery walls of the balloon and makes the water shoot out of the hole in the cap. Presto! You have squirtage with power—the power of air pressure.

# ping-pong airlines

How does a heavy airplane fly through thin air?

## WHAT DO YOU NEED?

- *A Ping-Pong ball*
- *The top part of your Pop Bottle*
- *A deep breath*

## WHAT DO YOU DO?

*1.* Place the ball inside the top part of your Pop Bottle and hold it with your finger.

*2.* Put your lips on the bottle's mouth. Purse your lips to get a nice solid stream of air. Blow into the mouth of the bottle so that your breath passes over the top of the ball.

*3.* Let go of the ball, but keep blowing. The ball should stay in place.

## WHAT'S GOING ON?

You just made one of the major scientific discoveries of all time. The faster air travels, the less pressure it exerts. In this experiment, your stream of breath decreased the pressure on top of the ball by making the air move at a faster rate. This made the slower-moving air under the ball more powerful. The air pressure under the ball didn't change, but the pressure now had more force than the air pressure on top. The pressure under the ball became so powerful, in fact, that the ball could defy gravity.

A plane's wing is designed so that air moves faster over the top of the wing than air passing underneath the wing. This causes a low-pressure zone above the wing and a high-pressure zone beneath. And just like your Ping-Pong ball, this gives airplanes the lift they need to fly through the air.

## flying bottle

### how can you make a pop bottle fly?

### WHAT DO YOU NEED?

■ *A pop bottle with the top and bottom cut off (and an adult to help you)— you should be left with a tube that's open at both ends*

■ *Paper clips*

### WHAT DO YOU DO?

*1.* Try throwing the tube. What happens?

*2.* Experiment by attaching paper clips to the tube. What happens when you place a lot of clips on the front end of the tube?

What about placing some clips on the back? How does your tube fly when you place the clips evenly apart?

*3.* Experiment with different kinds of throws. Does using a baseball throw work better than making a football throw and putting spin to it?

### WHAT'S GOING ON?

**P**aper clips allow the tube to glide through the air. The weight of the clips stabilizes the tube and keeps it from flipping end over end.

# soy sauce submarine

can you make a packet of soy sauce Rise and fall like a submarine?

### WHAT DO YOU NEED?

- *A plastic pop bottle*
- *Water*
- *Metal paper clips*
- *An unopened soy sauce packet—if you don't have one handy, you can use a ketchup packet or anything of that kind that is sealed in plastic*

## WHAT DO YOU DO?

*1.* Fill the bottle with tap water, leaving an inch or two empty at the top.

*2.* Put a metal paper clip on your soy sauce packet.

*3.* Poke the packet into the bottle. The packet should float, but it shouldn't ride too high above the water. If it bobs around too much, add a second paper clip.

*4.* Cap the bottle tightly.

*5.* Squeeze the bottle in the middle. You may need to give it a really good squeeze.

*6.* Watch the packet drop.

*7.* Let go and watch the packet rise.

## WHAT'S GOING ON?

A little pressure can do amazing things to air. In this experiment, when you squeezed the bottle, you compressed the little air pocket in the soy sauce packet. As the air particles were compressed, they became denser than water, and the packet sank. When you released the pressure, the air particles sprang back to normal, and the packet rose to the surface.

The secret ingredient in this experiment isn't soy sauce, it's water. Water can't be compressed as air can. Instead of shrinking when squeezed, the water made more room for itself in the bottle by compressing the air.

# metal boat

## can you make metal float?

### WHAT DO YOU NEED?

■ *Your Pop Bottle with the top part removed*
■ *Water*
■ *A bunch of pennies*
■ *A 12 x 12 inch square of aluminum foil*

### WHAT DO YOU DO?

*1.* Fill your Pop Bottle three-quarters full with water.

*2.* Drop one of the pennies into the bottle. Notice that a penny sinks; it doesn't float. (Take the penny out and dry it off.)

*3.* Take your aluminum foil square and fold all four corners into the center. Then fold the corners in again.

*4.* Mold the foil into a boat shape, making the sides high.

*5.* Place the boat on the water. It should float.

*6.* Take the penny that sank and place it in the boat. It should still float!

*7.* How many more pennies can you add before the boat sinks?

## WHAT'S GOING ON?

**Y**ou've just observed one of nature's most mysterious forces—the buoyant power of water.

Buoyancy is an upward force that causes objects to float and keeps things from sinking down into water. Not *all* objects, obviously. A boat that's been overloaded with pennies, or a boat that gets swamped with water, will sink. The power of buoyancy has limits. Often it is overwhelmed by another powerful force, the force of gravity, which pulls objects downward.

# density
# layer cake

### does the density of liquids affect buoyancy?

## WHAT DO YOU NEED?

- *Your Pop Bottle with the top part removed*
- *Water*
- *Objects to test: a grape, a paper clip, a cork, a pop bottle cap, a penny, and any other small objects you wish*
- *Measuring cup*
- *½ cup light corn syrup*

- *Food coloring (yellow and blue are good colors to use)*
- *½ cup olive oil or other cooking oil*
- *½ cup rubbing alcohol (have a grown-up help with this)*
- *Paper and a pen*

## WHAT DO YOU DO?

*1.* Fill the bottle about two-thirds full with water. Make sure the top part is removed.

*2.* Drop your objects in the water and make a note of which ones float and which ones sink.

*3.* Empty out your Pop Bottle.

*4.* Pour the syrup into your bottle.

*5.* Measure ½ cup water and add a drop or two of food coloring. Then slowly pour the water on top of the syrup, being careful not to mix the two.

*6.* Pour the oil on top of the water. If you've used the top part of the bottle as a funnel, rinse and dry it before pouring in the alcohol.

*7.* Get a grown-up to help you pour in the rubbing alcohol. (Caution: Alcohol is poisonous and should be used only with a grown-up present.)

*8.* Add a couple drops of food coloring to the rubbing alcohol.

**9.** Wait while the layers separate from each other and the colors mix in their layers.

**10.** Drop in some of your objects, and see where they land or float. Compare this with the notes you took earlier.

## WHAT'S GOING ON?

**Y**es, the density of liquids definitely affects buoyancy! Some objects may sink in water but won't sink to the bottom of this liquid layer cake.

# the magical floating egg

can you make an egg float in the middle of your pop bottle?

## WHAT DO YOU NEED?

- *Your Pop Bottle with the top part removed*
- *Water*
- *Two eggs*
- *Salt*

## WHAT DO YOU DO?

**1.** Fill your Pop Bottle about one-quarter full of water.

**2.** Break an uncooked egg into the water. It should sink.

*3.* Dump out the water and egg and fill the bottle about one-quarter full of water. Add salt and stir until the salt doesn't dissolve anymore. Break an egg into the salt water.

*4.* This is the tricky part. Slowly dribble water down the side of your Pop Bottle, being careful not to mix the fresh water with the salt water.

*5.* If the fresh water stays separate, the egg will float on top of the salt water and at the bottom of the fresh water.

## WHAT'S GOING ON?

**A**n egg will sink in fresh water but float in salt water. Fresh water is less dense than salt water (and less dense than an egg). If you pour fresh water in the ocean, it will float around on the surface until diffusion mixes the molecules and the fresh water becomes salt water.

# hard to change
### a neat trick

## WHAT DO YOU NEED?
- *An index card*
- *Your Pop Bottle with the top removed*
- *A quarter*

## WHAT DO YOU DO?

*1.* Place the index card on top of your Pop Bottle.

*2.* Place a quarter on the index card.

*3.* Flick the card with your finger so that the card flies out from under the quarter. The quarter should fall into the bottle.

*4.* Now invite someone else to try it. Say that they can have the quarter if they can flick the card and make the quarter fly across the room. Don't tell them exactly how it's done. It's fun to watch them figure it out!

## WHAT'S GOING ON?

**Y**ou demonstrated inertia, a property of all matter. Inertia is matter's tendency to remain at rest (even when the matter is made of billions and billions of moving molecules).

The energy source (your moving finger) acted upon the card but not the quarter. This experiment works because an index card is smooth and does not create much friction under the coin.

# bottle battle

## which two bottles can transfer the most energy?

### WHAT DO YOU NEED?

- *Two plastic pop bottles*
- *A hammer and nail to make holes in the caps (and an adult to help you)*
- *Two chairs with high backs*
- *Broom*
- *Duct tape or masking tape*
- *String cut into two 4-inch pieces and two 2-foot long pieces (The string must be strong enough to support the weight of a bottle filled with water.)*
- *Two pop bottle caps, each with two nail holes punched in the top*
- *Water*
- *A place outside for the battle*

## WHAT DO YOU DO?

*1.* Set up two chairs facing each other, about 3 to 4 feet apart.

*2.* Balance the broom handle on the backs of the chairs and tape the broom in place. (Test the chair surface with the tape first to be sure it won't harm the chair.)

*3.* Fill one pop bottle with water.

*4.* Thread the two short pieces of string through the holes in your bottle caps. Knot the ends of the string so that the string forms a loop. Put the caps on the bottles and test the strength of the string over a sink.

*5.* Tie one long string to each of the string loops in the bottle caps. Test the strings' strength.

*6.* Tie the ends of the long strings to the broom handle so that the bottles hang straight down. They should be about a foot apart.

*7.* Hold the empty pop bottle away from the full one and let it go. What happens?

*8.* Hold the full bottle away from the empty bottle and let it go. What happens?

**9.** Now fill the empty bottle up to the same level as the full bottle. What happens when two full bottles collide?

## WHAT'S GOING ON?

**T**he biggest transfer of energy occurred when a full bottle struck an empty bottle. The least amount of energy was transferred when the empty bottle struck the full bottle. The two full bottles transferred energy back and forth each time they collided. They lost a little energy with each swing (due to air friction and gravity), until the bottles stopped swinging altogether.

# pop bottle derby

## challenge your family and friends!

## WHAT DO YOU NEED FOR A RACER?

- *Cardboard*
- *A plastic pop bottle*
- *Hot glue gun (and an adult to help you use it)*
- *A straw (wider than ⅛ inch)*
- *2 wooden dowels (⅛ inch in diameter)*

- *4 plastic pop bottle caps*
- *A racecourse that includes a ramp and goal line*

## WHAT DO YOU AND YOUR GROWN-UP HELPER DO?

**1.** Cut a cardboard base for the bottle. The base can be any size or shape you wish.

**2.** Glue the base to the bottle with the hot glue gun.

**3.** Cut the straw into two 3-inch lengths. These will be used as axle holders. Glue the straws to the bottom of the cardboard. One piece of straw should be in the front and one should be in the back. Both should be centered.

**4.** Cut the wooden dowels to use as axles. Secure each axle to the racer by running it through the axle holder.

**5.** Make wheels by securing bottle caps with glue to the end of each axle.

## AND YOU'RE OFF!

**1.** See how far you can make a racer travel.

**2.** Harness the power of gravity. Make a

ramp and experiment with the angle of the ramp's incline. Add objects to the bottle and see if weight makes a difference.

*3.* Try different materials for the ramp itself. Does a smooth or rough ramp make the car go farther?

*4.* Challenge friends and family to a Pop Bottle Race! Whose racer will go the fastest or the farthest? Set up a racecourse with a goal line, and see whose racer gets there first.

# Plasts, Bangs, Twists, and Other Reactions

## disappearing eggshell
### which liquid will dissolve the shell?

**WHAT DO YOU NEED?**

- Your Pop Bottle without the top
- Vinegar
- Bowl (or a second pop bottle)
- Water
- Two hard-boiled eggs with their shells on

## WHAT DO YOU DO?

*1.* Fill your Pop Bottle about three-quarters full of vinegar.

*2.* Fill the second bottle or bowl about three-quarters full of water.

*3.* Take a guess: Which of the two liquids can dissolve the eggshells?

*4.* Gently drop one hard-boiled egg into the vinegar in your Pop Bottle. The eggs should fizz.

*5.* Gently drop the other hard-boiled egg into the water.

*6.* Leave the eggs in the vinegar and water for one to two days.

*7.* Which liquid dissolves eggshells?

## WHAT'S GOING ON?

**V**inegar is an acid. It can dissolve chemicals such as calcium. Water cannot; water doesn't contain acid. Since an eggshell is mostly made of calcium, vinegar will dissolve the shell. The vinegar is now a solution of vinegar and calcium. If you let the vinegar evaporate, calcium crystals would be left behind.

## KEEP GOING!

**V**inegar can also take the calcium out of bones. To see this for yourself, clean a chicken bone (a wishbone is the most fun) and let it dry overnight. Soak the bone in vinegar for a week. You can take the bone out of the vinegar and check it every day, if you want. By the end of the week, the bone will be so bendy, you can tie it in a knot.

# cabbage juice

make COLORs change as if by magic.

## WHAT DO YOU NEED?

- *A head of purple cabbage*
- *Saucepan, stove, and a grown-up to help out with chopping and boiling*
- *Strainer or sieve*
- *Your Pop Bottle with the top part removed*
- *2 glasses*
- *Paper and a pencil*
- *White vinegar*
- *Baking soda*

## WHAT DO YOU DO?

*1.* Chop up a head of purple cabbage as finely as possible.

*2.* Heat about 4 cups of water in a saucepan. Add the cabbage to the boiling water.

*3.* Simmer for 10 minutes, and then remove the pan from the heat.

*4.* Wait until the cabbage cools down.

*5.* Pour the liquid through a strainer into your Pop Bottle. This is your cabbage juice.

*6.* Discard the cabbage (or serve it with dinner).

*7.* Set the empty glasses side by side.

*8.* In one glass, pour about 1 inch of vinegar. Use the paper and pencil to label this glass VINEGAR.

*9.* In the other glass, pour about 3 tablespoons of baking soda. Label it SODA.

*10.* Pour a small amount of the cabbage juice into each glass (the baking soda will need to be stirred) until you see the color change.

## WHAT'S GOING ON?

The technical name for the cabbage juice is an *indicator.* In science labs, the juice indicates whether a substance is an acid, a base (also known as an *alkaline*), or a neutral.

- Acids and cabbage juice make a red mixture.

- Bases and cabbage juice make a green or greenish-blue mixture.

- Neutrals and cabbage juice don't change color much at all.

What happened in your glass of vinegar? How about your glass of baking soda? Which one is a base and which one is an acid?

Test other substances around your house.

# raisin water ballet

watch the dancing Raisins do their stuff.

## WHAT DO YOU NEED?

- ■ *Your Pop Bottle with the top part removed*
- ■ *Water*
- ■ *Vinegar*
- ■ *Baking soda*
- ■ *10 raisins*

## WHAT DO YOU DO?

*1.* Fill your Pop Bottle about halfway with water.

**2.** Pour in 4 tablespoons of vinegar.

**3.** Add 3 tablespoons of baking soda. (The mixture will begin to fizz.)

**4.** Drop in the raisins. They may sink initially, but will soon bounce around in the bottle.

## WHAT'S GOING ON?

The vinegar and baking soda create carbon dioxide bubbles, the same gas that carbonates soda pop. Bubbles will gather under the raisins until there's enough fizz to raise the raisins to the surface. There, the bubbles burst, and the raisins sink back down.

## HAVE SOME CLEANING TO DO?

The vinegar and baking soda mixture makes a super cleanser. Try it (without the raisins) on the kitchen or bathroom sink and see.

# gas balloon
## an acid and a base make gas.

### WHAT DO YOU NEED?
- *A plastic pop bottle*
- *White vinegar*
- *Baking soda*
- *Paper towel (If your brand is the super-duper absorbent kind, try a few layers of toilet tissue instead.)*
- *Balloon*

### WHAT DO YOU DO?

*1.* Fill your bottle half full of white vinegar.

*2.* Put about 1 tablespoon of baking soda into a paper towel and wrap it up to make a tightly wrapped packet.

*3.* Poke the baking soda packet into the bottle so that it falls into the vinegar.

*4.* Quickly put the balloon over the mouth of the bottle and set the bottle on the counter.

## WHAT'S GOING ON?

**W**hen vinegar comes into contact with baking soda, the reaction produces a gas called *carbon dioxide*. The gas has fast-moving molecules that take up a lot of space and expand—blowing up the balloon.

# pop boat

## Launch a bottle on water.

## WHAT DO YOU NEED?

- *A plastic pop bottle and cap*
- *A hammer and nail (and an adult to help out)*
- *Vinegar*
- *Optional: A marble or small stone*
- *Baking soda*
- *Paper towel*
- *Bathtub full of water or an area outside where you can launch your boat*

## WHAT DO YOU DO?

*1.* Get a grown-up to help you put a hole in the cap of a pop bottle.

**2.** Fill the bottle half full with vinegar.

**3.** Optional: Drop in a marble or small stone.

**4.** Wrap a tablespoon of baking soda tightly in a paper towel.

**5.** Put the paper towel packet in the pop bottle and tighten the cap quickly.

**6.** Place the bottle on its side in the water.

**7.** Optional: Slide the marble or stone into the bottle's neck, so that the weight keeps the cap in the water.

**8.** Let go. Your bottle boat should zip forward in the water.

## WHAT'S GOING ON?

When acids and bases come together in a confined space, the results can be powerful. In this experiment, the vinegar and baking soda create carbon dioxide gas that propels the boat in the water.

# cork rocket
## blast off!

### WHAT DO YOU NEED?

- *A plastic pop bottle*
- *White vinegar*
- *Baking soda*
- *Paper towels*
- *Open space*
- *Cork (or use clay to make a plug)*
- *A grown-up to help out*

### WHAT DO YOU DO?

*1.* Fill the pop bottle half full of white vinegar.

*2.* Put a tablespoon of baking soda into a paper towel and wrap it up to make a tightly wrapped packet.

*3.* Take the bottle and cork outside where you have some space and drop the baking soda packet into the bottle.

*4.* Quickly plug the bottle with the cork. Make sure the seal is tight, set the bottle on the ground, and back away to a safe distance.

## WHAT'S GOING ON?

**A**s the vinegar soaks through the paper towel packet, it slowly comes into contact with the baking soda and begins to create carbon dioxide gas. This gas builds and builds until it is so crammed in the bottle that it pushes out the cork and launches it into flight!

# air crunch

use the power of a storm to crush a bottle.

## WHAT DO YOU NEED?

- A sink or a bowl
- Ice and cold water
- Hot tap water
- Plastic pop bottle with cap

## WHAT DO YOU DO?

**1.** Fill a bowl (one that's large enough for the pop bottle to fit inside) with ice and cold water.

**2.** Run the tap water until it gets extremely hot and fill up your pop bottle. Let the bottle sit for about 1 minute so that the bottle heats up.

*3.* Dump out the hot water and put the cap on *immediately.* You want to trap as much of the hot air (especially the steamy water vapor) as possible.

*4.* Put the bottle in the ice bath and hold it under water. (If the cold water bothers your hands, hold it under with some kitchen tongs.)

*5.* Wait a few seconds and see what happens to the bottle.

## WHAT'S GOING ON?

Hot air creates a lot of air pressure. But as water vapor condenses, and turns from gas back into liquid, the pressure decreases. In this experiment, you made the pressure inside the bottle decrease *very* rapidly when you plunged the bottle into cold water. Colder air outside the bottle pushed against and gave it a crunch.

If you watch weather reports, you'll notice that high and low pressure areas are a big part of the report. Generally speaking, high pressure means good weather. Low pressure can mean rain. And when the two types of pressure collide, there could be some rough weather.

People in the eastern United States particularly experience this in the form of storms called nor'easters, when low pressure systems traveling up from Florida hit high pressure systems traveling down from the Arctic.

# underwater crunch

TRy This the next time you'Re in a swimming pool.

## WHAT DO YOU NEED?

- *An empty plastic pop bottle with cap on*
- *A pool with a deep end of at least 5 feet*
- *A swimmer (you) and a grown-up if you're not allowed in the pool alone*

## WHAT DO YOU DO?

*1.* Grab an empty pop bottle, tighten the cap, and hop into the pool.

*2.* Swim down to the bottom of the pool. What happens to the bottle?

## WHAT'S GOING ON?

**W**ater pressure crushed your bottle. Underwater, you can feel the pressure as it pushes on you from every angle. The weight of the water from all sides increases as you go deeper. Just be glad you're not made of plastic and empty like your bottle!

# crystals

## gROW SaLT cRYSTaLS in WaTeR.

### WHAT DO YOU NEED?

- *Your Pop Bottle without the top*
- *Hot tap water*
- *Salt*
- *String*
- *A ruler*
- *A nail*

### WHAT DO YOU DO?

*1.* Fill the bottle about half full of hot tap water.

*2.* Add salt to the water and stir. Keep adding salt and stirring until you see salt at the bottom of the bottle. (This means the water can't absorb any more salt.)

*3.* Tie one end of the string around the middle of the ruler. The ruler will be laid across the opening at the top of the bottle so that the string and nail can dangle into the water.

**4.** Tie the other end of the string around the head of the nail. Measure the string length so that the nail comes close to, but doesn't touch, the bottom of the bottle. Cut off any extra string.

**5.** Set the ruler across the bottle opening and position the dangling string and nail in the middle of the bottom. You should start to see crystals in a few days.

### WHAT'S GOING ON?

In this experiment, the water is known as a saturated solution. The water is saturated with salt. As the water evaporates, the salt is left behind. The abandoned salt molecules cling together and grab on to the string, making crystals that are shaped like little cubes. In a few days the water totally evaporates, and you're left with a string of salt crystals.

# volcano!
*design your own.*

### WHAT DO YOU NEED?

- *White vinegar*
- *A plastic pop bottle*
- *⅓ cup dishwashing liquid*
- *Red food coloring*
- *Duct tape or masking tape*
- *A piece of cardboard roughly 9 x 12 inches*
- *Newspaper*

- *Aluminum foil*
- *Baking soda*
- *Paper towel*
- *Optional: ¼ cup glitter and ¼ cup sand. You can also toss in some grains of Tang, Kool-Aid, or other powdered red or orange fruit drink.*

## WHAT DO YOU DO?

### Build the volcano:

**1.** Pour about ½ cup of white vinegar into the bottle.

**2.** Add ⅓ cup of dishwashing liquid.

**3.** Add a few drops of red food coloring.

**4.** Make sure the bottom of the bottle is dry. Tape down your Pop Bottle in the center of the cardboard.

**5.** Ball up newspapers, and tape them around the bottle to build up a mountain-like shape. The mouth of the bottle should be slightly higher than the newspaper.

**6.** Place a sheet of aluminum foil over the bottle and the newspaper. Smooth it down.

**7.** Use your finger to poke through the foil into the mouth of the bottle. The bottle mouth should be completely open.

**For the eruption:**

*1.* Wrap 1 tablespoon of baking soda in a paper towel.

*2.* Put the baking soda packet into the bottle and *stand back!*

### WHAT'S GOING ON?

The baking soda and vinegar create carbon dioxide gas in the bottle. As the gas expands, there is suddenly not enough room in the bottle. The only place for the gas to go is out through the mouth of the bottle.

Just as with a real volcano, the expanding gas in a confined space was powerful enough to cause an eruption. As the gas blows out, it forces some of the bottle's contents to flow like lava down a mountainside.

# twister!

see how Twisters work.

### WHAT DO YOU NEED?

- Waterproof glue
- 2 pop bottle caps
- A nail and a hammer to make holes in the caps (and a grown-up to help you)

- Two 2-liter plastic pop bottles
- Water
- Duct tape or black electrician's tape

## WHAT DO YOU DO?

*1.* Using waterproof glue, stick the two caps together, top to top.

*2.* Wait until the glue dries, then use the hammer and nail to make a hole through both caps.

*3.* Fill one bottle about three-quarters full with water and screw on the cap.

*4.* Screw the other bottle on the other side of the cap.

*5.* The two bottles should now look like an elongated figure eight. Wrap duct or electrician's tape around the middle joint so that the space between the two caps is sealed. Your Tornado Maker is now complete.

*6.* Flip the Tornado Maker over so that the water-filled bottle is on top. Grasp the joint in the middle and swirl the Tornado Maker in a circle. Watch for the vortex to appear. Then turn the bottle over and repeat.

## WHAT'S GOING ON?

**A**s you swirl the Tornado Maker, the water in the bottle forms a spiral. This spiral shape has a hole in the middle and air rushes upward to fill the hole. This, in turn, creates room in the lower bottle for water to travel down. Soon, air and water are

rushing past each other as air bubbles up and water pours down.

How is this like a tornado? The spiraling funnel of a tornado is created by the swirling energy of rapidly rising hot air and rapidly falling cold air.

# smoke launcher

## shoot a vortex.

### WHAT DO YOU NEED?

- *Scissors*
- *A balloon*
- *The top part of your Pop Bottle*
- *A rubber band*
- *A candle and matches and a grown-up to help you light candles and make smoke*

### WHAT DO YOU DO?

*1.* Cut the neck off a balloon. Then stretch your balloon like a shower cap over the wide part of your Pop Bottle top.

*2.* Place the rubber band around the rim to keep the balloon on tight. This is now your Smoke Launcher.

*3.* Light a candle and then blow it out. Collect the smoke in your Smoke Launcher by holding the small open end over the smoking wick.

*4.* Light the candle again. Step back a few feet from the candle.

*5.* Aim your Smoke Launcher at the flame and gently tap the balloon. If the smoke is a gray blur, you're tapping too hard. You should see spinning smoke rings.

*6.* When you hit the candle, it will put out the flame, and you'll see a smoke ring form on the other side of the candle.

*7.* Try a smoke ring trick. Shoot a slow ring and then shoot a faster one. If your aim and timing are just right, the faster ring can pass through the slower one.

### WHAT'S GOING ON?

When you tap your launcher, smoke is pushed through the bottle opening. The air moving directly against the bottle's inner surface is slowed down by friction. The air in the middle of the opening moves more quickly. This difference in speed causes the air to rotate from the center of the opening to the edge, and this rotation creates a vortex.

The higher speed at the center also creates a pressure difference in the smoke. The faster-moving center has a lower pressure than the air at the edge. This imbalance in pressure helps keep the vortex rolling until it finally runs out of energy and disappears.

# Secrets of Earth and Space

## sky colors

see why the sky looks blue in the day and red at sunset.

### WHAT DO YOU NEED?

- *Your Pop Bottle without the top*
- *Water*
- *Milk*
- *Flashlight*
- *A darkened room*

### WHAT DO YOU DO?

*1.* Fill the bottle about two-thirds full of water.

*2.* Add 1 teaspoon of milk to the water and stir.

**3.** Take the bottle and a flashlight into a darkened room.

**4.** Put the bottle on the floor and shine the flashlight straight down into it. The mixture should have a slight blue tint.

**5.** Shine the flashlight toward the side of the bottle. The mixture should now have a slight red tint.

**6.** Shine the flashlight under the bottle while looking straight down into the bottle. The mixture should have a deeper red tint.

## WHAT'S GOING ON?

**L**ight is made up of many colors. You see this principle in a rainbow. In this experiment, small particles of milk, floating throughout the water, scattered the beam of light from the flashlight. When this happened, the light seemed to change color.

This happens, on a larger scale and with more vivid colors, in our atmosphere. Dust particles and air molecules scatter light from the sun. As the earth's rotation affects the direction of the sunlight, we see different colors in our sky.

# make a compass
## which way is north?

### WHAT DO YOU NEED?
- *Your Pop Bottle without the top*
- *Water*
- *Dishwashing liquid*
- *Your Pop Bottle cap*
- *Bar magnet*
- *Needle*

### WHAT DO YOU DO?

*1.* Fill your Pop Bottle about three-quarters full of water.

*2.* Add a drop of dishwashing liquid to the water.

*3.* Float your cap like a small boat in the water, with the inside of the cap facing up.

*4.* Magnetize your needle. To do this, rub your magnet in one direction and in one smooth motion from the eye of the needle to the needle tip. It's important to only go in one direction—eye to point. Do this about 20 times.

*5.* *Carefully* float the needle on the cap. What happens?

### WHAT'S GOING ON?

It might spin a little, but in the end the needle should point north. How come?

Magnets have two kinds of charges: one is positive, and the other is negative. In magnetism, opposites always attract. A positive charge, in other words, will always be attracted to a negative charge and vice versa.

Our planet Earth is a gigantic magnet, with a north pole and a south pole. When you placed the magnetized needle on the water, it oriented itself to the magnetic field of the earth. The needle's positive charges all pointed toward the tip, so the needle pointed to Earth's giant negative charge, the north pole.

# earth shake

Want to see what kind of dirt you have around you? the best way to do that is to shake things up.

## WHAT DO YOU NEED?
■ *A plastic pop bottle*
■ *Soil*
■ *Water*

## WHAT DO YOU DO?

*1.* Fill the bottle about half full of soil from a single source.

*2.* Fill the rest of the bottle with water and put the cap on it.

*3.* Shake the bottle for several minutes. Then let it sit on the counter.

*4.* Watch what happens when the water clears.

## WHAT'S GOING ON?

**Y**ou made a mixture of water and soil, which allowed the different components of soil to shake out according to their density. Denser objects sink to the bottom while less dense materials may float on top. The size of your layers may differ wildly, depending on where you take your samples, but the pattern will always be the same. Take another bottle and repeat this experiment with soil from a completely different source. Try a forest or a beach.

## WANT TO GET GEOLOGICAL?

Take a look at your layers.

**Pebbles**—Rocks are the densest parts of most soil samples. They sink to the bottom.

**Sand**—Sand is made up of grains of rock—smaller than pebbles, but big enough to sink in most soil samples.

**Silt**—Silt is very fine sand.

**Muddy water**—Particles that can neither sink nor float settle in a layer of water and make it cloudy. These particles will eventually settle.

**Floating things**—Dead leaves, sticks, bugs, and other organic material that can float make up the top layer. In nature, these materials are extremely nutrient rich and help feed plants.

# the shape of our galaxy

what shapes our galaxy into a spiral?

## WHAT DO YOU NEED?

- *Your Pop Bottle without the top*
- *Water*
- *Dried herbs such as oregano, parsley, or thyme—any bits of dried leaves that float*
- *A pencil or chopstick*

## WHAT DO YOU DO?

*1.* Fill your Pop Bottle about half full with water.

*2.* Sprinkle 1 tablespoon of dried herbs on top.

*3.* Stir the water in one direction with your pencil or chopstick.

*4.* Once the water is going fast enough, take the stirrer out and watch the motion of the herbs.

## WHAT'S GOING ON?

The herbs swirl around a vortex, just like the material in our galaxy. Many kinds of vortices occur in nature. A whirlpool, a tornado, the water draining out of your tub, weather systems, our own galaxy—all of these natural phenomenal are shaped in a spiral by a vortex.

A vortex draws things toward the center, and the spiral spin keeps a collision from occurring. Our galaxy, the Milky Way, is a spiral with several arms swirling around its hub.

By the way, it takes Earth 200,000,000 years to make a full circle around the hub of the Milky Way. Scientists are still trying to find out what's in the hub of our galaxy. Some scientists believe that the hub is packed with exploding and collapsing stars.

# marble earth
## why doesn't the earth fly into the sun?

### WHAT DO YOU NEED?
- *A marble*
- *Your Pop Bottle*

### WHAT DO YOU DO?

*1.* Pop the marble into your Pop Bottle and close it tight (use tape or another bottle if it's loose).

*2.* Swirl the marble in a clockwise direction until it creeps up the wall of the bottle.

### WHAT'S GOING ON?

The force that keeps Earth from flying into the sun is the same force that keeps the marble on the sides of the Pop Bottle. It is called *centrifugal force*. If not for that force, the earth *would* fly into the sun.

The marble stayed in orbit because of the sides of the bottle. Similarly, the gravitational pull of the sun keeps the earth in place. The speed of the marble keeps it racing around the center of the bottle. Similarly, the speed of Earth's orbit (an average velocity of approximately 30,000 meters per second) keeps it from getting any closer to the sun. The effect of the sun's gravitational pull on our planet is offset by the centrifugal force generated during Earth's orbit.

# moon surface
## how did the moon get craters?

### WHAT DO YOU NEED?

- *2 cups of flour*
- *Your Pop Bottle without the top*
- *A place outside—or, if you're doing this inside, newspapers to spread on the floor*
- *Small objects: raisins, grapes, chocolate chips, or beads*

### WHAT DO YOU DO?

*1.* Gently place the flour in the bottle and tap the sides of the bottle so the surface is smooth.

*2.* Place the bottle on the ground or on the newspapers.

*3.* Stand above the bottle and drop your objects onto the flour. Lob one of them gently. Toss one a little harder. What do you see?

## WHAT'S GOING ON?

**W**hen our solar system was forming, bits of debris bombarded the planets and moons, creating deep craters. Our planet was probably covered with craters, but, due to geological changes, including erosion caused by the atmosphere, the earth's surface was transformed over millions of years.

The moon has no atmosphere. It has no storms and no wind or rain to erode the surface and change the landscape. While our planet has always been changing, the moon's surface looks the same as it did when it first got banged up millions of years ago.

# cosmic spot

## can you Re-cReate jupiteR's Red spot?

### WHAT DO YOU NEED?

- *1 cup of whole milk*
- *Your Pop Bottle without the top*
- *Red and yellow food coloring*
- *Dishwashing detergent*

### WHAT DO YOU DO?

*1.* Pour the cup of milk in the bottle.

*2.* Place one dot each of red and yellow food coloring on the surface of the milk.

*3.* Gently swirl the bottle to move the dots.

*4.* Place one drop of dishwashing liquid on each of the color spots.

*5.* Keep swirling, and watch the storm brew.

### WHAT'S GOING ON?

The swirls in your Pop Bottle are a model of the Red Spot on Jupiter. When you swirl the milk, you create something called a pattern of flow. These are just like the patterns caused by the winds that blow over the surface of a planet.

The spot we see on Jupiter is a huge storm system of heated gases that swirl around at incredible speeds. The Red Spot is a storm that has been raging on Jupiter for at least as long as scientists have been observing the planet—more than three hundred years!

# Bottled Weather

## Hot stuff

### Where does hot water travel?

### WHAT DO YOU NEED?

- 2 sturdy, 1-liter plastic bottles
- Hot and cold water
- Dark food coloring
- A playing card or index card

### WHAT DO YOU DO?

Fill one bottle up to the top with cold water. Put a few drops of food coloring in the other bottle and add hot tap water—as hot as you can get it without melting the bottle or burning yourself. Set this bottle on the counter or in the sink.

Place the card over the opening of the cold water bottle and carefully flip it over. Place the cold water bottle on top of the hot water bottle so that their mouths are lined up, and slide the card out.

### WHAT'S GOING ON?

**Y**ou should see the colored water rising from the bottom bottle into the top bottle. Since cold water is denser, it sinks and pushes the hot water beneath it upward.

This hot and cold exchange happens with air, as well. This is called *convection*, and it affects our weather and how heat is moved around the planet.

# rainmaker

## discover the process that makes rain.

### WHAT DO YOU NEED?

- *Your Pop Bottle*
- *Hot tap water*
- *Ice*

## WHAT DO YOU DO?

*1.* Take the top part off your Pop Bottle, leaving the cap screwed on tightly.

*2.* Fill the bottom part of the Pop Bottle half full of hot tap water.

*3.* Turn the top part of the bottle so it's upside down and fill it with ice. Set this into the bottom part of the Pop Bottle and wait.

*4.* What do you notice?

## WHAT'S GOING ON?

You created a miniature water cycle in your bottle. The cycle consists of *evaporation*, *condensation*, and *precipitation*.

Evaporation turns liquid water into a water vapor gas that rises into the air. Heat causes the water to evaporate.

As the vapor cools, it turns back into a liquid. This is called condensation. In your Pop Bottle, the water vapor rises until it reaches the cold zone caused by the ice. You can see droplets forming and hanging from the plastic. In nature, condensed water vapor shows up in our sky as clouds.

Clouds in the sky collect water droplets until all the droplets are too heavy to float in the air. Then water falls from the sky as rain. This is called precipitation. In your Pop Bottle, the droplets get heavier and heavier until they fall back down into the bottom part of the bottle.

# bottle cloud

can you discover what clouds are made of?

## WHAT DO YOU NEED?

- *Black construction paper*
- *Hot tap water*
- *A plastic pop bottle*
- *Matches (and an adult to help you)*

## WHAT DO YOU DO?

*1.* Prop up the black construction paper on your kitchen counter. You will use the paper as a background later on.

*2.* Turn on the hot water tap at your sink. Wait until the water is very hot. For safety, turn the water back to a strong dribble and dribble about 2 inches of very hot water into the bottle.

*3.* Blow into the bottle opening to put pressure on the water. (The bottle must be fully expanded.) Quickly cap the bottle.

*4.* Now start shaking! Shake the bottle for about 1 minute. This will mix the water vapor molecules with the air.

*5.* Put the bottle on the counter. Have a grown-up strike a match. Let it burn for about 2 seconds. Blow out the match.

Quickly uncap the bottle, drop in the match, and quickly cap up the bottle again.

**6.** Lay the bottle on its side in front of the black paper. (The dark paper makes the cloud easier to see.) Press on the side of the bottle as hard as you can for about 10 seconds. Let go and see if you have a cloud. If not, repeat this until you see a cloud form in the bottle.

**7.** When you see a cloud, remove the bottle cap. The cloud may leave the bottle on its own. If not, give the cloud a push by lightly squeezing the bottle.

### WHAT'S GOING ON?

Clouds are made of water vapor, air, and particles of dust. In this experiment, the cloud began forming in the bottle when particles from the smoky, sooty match attached themselves to the water vapor in the air.

# dew point
where does condensation come from?

## WHAT DO YOU NEED?
- *Your Pop Bottle without the top part*
- *Warm water*
- *Ice cubes*
- *A spoon*

## WHAT DO YOU DO?

*1.* Fill your Pop Bottle about two-thirds full of warm tap water.

*2.* Add ice cubes one at a time and stir the water with the spoon until the cubes melt.

*3.* Touch the outside of the bottle. Wait a few minutes and touch it again. What happens?

## WHAT'S GOING ON?

The condensation on a glass comes from the outside air, not the water inside. The air all around us is filled with particles of warm water vapor. These water vapor particles will turn back into liquid on any surface that has cooled below a certain temperature.

This liquid water is dew. The dew point is when water vapor in the air is cool enough to turn into liquid water. Dew forms on the grass in the same way.

# pop bottle barometer

Can you make a device to measure differences in air pressure?

## WHAT DO YOU NEED?

- *Scissors*
- *A balloon*
- *Your Pop Bottle without the top part*
- *A rubber band*
- *Two straws*
- *A toothpick*
- *A ruler*
- *A marker*
- *Paper and a pen*
- *Tape*
- *A place where you can leave your barometer to make its measurements (The place should have a fairly constant temperature.)*

## WHAT DO YOU DO?

*1.* Cut the neck off the balloon. Secure the top tightly to the opening of your Pop Bottle with a rubber band. (If you find that the barometer doesn't work, try strengthening the seal by pulling the balloon tighter.)

*2.* Tape the two straws together and make one long straw.

**3.** Tape the toothpick to one end of the long straw so that the toothpick can work as a pointer. Tape the other end of the long straw to the center of the balloon. The straw should stick out about 6 inches from the bottle.

**4.** Now make a measurement chart. Line up the bottom of a ruler with a piece of paper and mark quarter-inch increments from the bottom of the paper to the top. Label each increment: 1, 1¼, 1½, 1¾, 2, and so forth.

**5.** Tape the completed measurement chart to the wall behind the barometer. Position the barometer and the chart, so that the toothpick points at a number near the middle of the chart.

**6.** On your paper, record the date, what the weather is like, and the number that the toothpick points to.

**7.** Record readings every day (especially when there's a change in the weather). Can you see a pattern?

## WHAT'S GOING ON?

When the toothpick points at high numbers, air pressure is pushing down on the balloon. When the toothpick points at lower numbers, there is little air pressure pushing on the balloon.

You should discover a connection between your barometer's readings and the weather. On sunny, clear days, the reading should be high. High pressure (as weather people call it) means the atmosphere is thicker over your area, and that usually means good weather. On stormy days, the reading should be lower because there is usually low pressure when it rains.

# pop bottle thermometer

*Can you make a device to measure temperature?*

## WHAT DO YOU NEED?

- ■ *Food coloring*
- ■ *A sturdy, 1-liter plastic bottle*
- ■ *Water*
- ■ *A clear straw*
- ■ *Modeling clay (plasticine works well)*
- ■ *An index card and a pen*
- ■ *An outdoor thermometer to calibrate your homemade version*

## WHAT DO YOU DO?

*1.* Drip two drops of food coloring (preferably red) into your bottle.

*2.* Fill the pop bottle with warm water. Leave about 2 inches of space at the top of the bottle.

*3.* Place the straw in the bottle so it hangs a little lower than halfway down. The straw should stick out about 4 inches above the bottle.

**4.** Use the modeling clay to hold the straw in place. The water level in the straw should be about 2 inches from the mouth of the bottle, about halfway up the straw. There should be no air spaces between the straw and the mouth of the bottle. If your thermometer doesn't work, check this seal.

**5.** Tape an index card to the straw and make a mark on the card to record the current water level.

**6.** Take your thermometer to a sunny spot and let it sit for about an hour.

**7.** Check your thermometer and mark the water level. Check an outdoor thermometer and see what temperature it is reading. Put that number next to the water level mark.

**8.** Read your thermometer every day, and check it against the regular thermometer to test its accuracy.

## WHAT'S GOING ON?

**A**s the temperature increases, a liquid will expand. This is the working principle of a thermometer. In your homemade version, heat causes the water to expand up the straw. The hotter the temperature gets, the higher the water rises and the higher the thermometer reading will be.

# warm and warmer

## which heats up more quickly—land or water?

## WHAT DO YOU NEED?

- *2 plastic pop bottles with their tops removed*
- *Soil*
- *Water*
- *2 thermometers*
- *A lamp with a 60-watt bulb or higher (or a sunny windowsill)*
- *Tape*
- *Paper and a pen*

## WHAT DO YOU DO?

*1.* Fill one bottle three-quarters full of dirt.

*2.* Fill the other three-quarters full of water.

*3.* Tape a thermometer inside each bottle so that the bottoms of the thermometers are buried in either dirt or water. Wait several minutes and then record the temperatures both thermometers are reading.

*4.* Place a lamp over both bottles. The lamp should be shining an equal distance from both bottles. (Alternatively, you could use a sunny windowsill.)

**5.** Record the temperatures every 5 minutes for about an hour.

**6.** What do you notice?

**7.** Turn off the lamp and record the temperatures in the same time intervals. Which cools off more quickly?

## WHAT'S GOING ON?

**Y**our temperature readings should show that the soil heated up much faster than water. It takes more energy from the sun to heat the water molecules enough to raise the temperature. Soil, on the other hand, contains many air pockets and is less dense than water. The sun heats soil more quickly.

When it comes to cooling, soil cools down faster than water as well. The next time you are at the beach in summer, test it with your feet. If it's been hot all day, the sand will be hot. But after the sun goes down, the sand will cool off, while the water will still be warm—in fact, you may be surprised how chilly you feel when you come out of the water.

# Plants and Other Living Things

## green leaf, red leaf

### why do Leaves change COLOR?

**WHAT DO YOU NEED?**
- 3 fresh, juicy, green leaves
- A coffee filter paper, cut into a strip 1 inch wide and about 6 inches long, and with one end cut into a point
- A pencil
- Rubbing alcohol
- Your Pop Bottle without the top part
- Tape
- A ruler
- Plastic wrap

## WHAT DO YOU DO?

*1.* Place one of the leaves on the coffee filter paper about ½ inch up from the point. Using the pencil eraser, press down on the leaf so it makes a green streak on the paper.

*2.* Let the paper dry (if need be).

*3.* In the same place on the paper, make another green streak from another leaf. Do this three times altogether with three different, fresh, leaves.

*4.* Have a grown-up help you pour about 1 inch of rubbing alcohol into your Pop Bottle.

*5.* Tape the paper strip to a ruler. Hang the strip of paper point side down so that just the tip touches the rubbing alcohol. The green streak should not touch the alcohol itself. (If you find that the paper is too short, either add another length of paper to the ruler at the top or add more alcohol to the bottle.)

*6.* Cover the bottle opening with plastic wrap so the alcohol won't evaporate.

*7.* Wait approximately 30 minutes.

*8.* What happens to the green?

## WHAT'S GOING ON?

**T**he green pigment in leaves is called *chlorophyll*. But chlorophyll isn't the only pigment in the leaves. Other color pigments are there, as well. You can see these other colors in the fall when the chlorophyll breaks down and reveals the other pigments in the leaf.

Those other pigments are also revealed in this experiment. The alcohol separates the color pigments from one another as the liquid moves up the paper strip.

# pop bottle garden

### can you sprout a dried bean into a live plant?

## WHAT DO YOU NEED?

- *White paper towel*
- *Water*
- *Uncooked dried beans (lima beans work well)*
- *Your Pop Bottle with the top removed*

## WHAT DO YOU DO?

*1.* Soak the white paper towel in water. Squeeze the towel to remove excess water. The towel should be damp but not dripping.

*2.* Place the beans in the paper towel and cover them.

*3.* Keep the paper damp. Check your beans every day.

*4.* What happens?

## WHAT'S GOING ON?

**T**he beans you sprouted only need water to grow. They don't even need dirt at first. When your sprouts get big enough, though, you might plant them in dirt and see if you can grow big plants.

# vegetable in a bottle

## can you grow a vegetable inside a bottle?

## WHAT DO YOU NEED?

- A garden that includes a vegetable plant with buds
- A plastic pop bottle
- String

## WHAT DO YOU DO?

*1.* Find a healthy-looking blossom on a vegetable plant such as a squash or a cucumber.

*2.* Place the blossom inside the pop bottle, without separating the blossom from the plant.

*3.* Gently tie a string around the neck of the pop bottle and the plant stem so the blossom won't move out of the bottle.

*4.* Wait for a few weeks, and see what happens inside your bottle.

### WHAT'S GOING ON?

**W**ith luck and patience, you can grow a full-size vegetable inside your pop bottle! The plastic is transparent, so sunlight still reaches the fruit, but the important thing is that sunlight reaches the leaves of the plant. The leaves are the food factories for any plant—taking sunshine and changing it into sugars for the plant to use for growing.

# flower power
## how do plants get water from the soil?

### WHAT DO YOU NEED?
- *Food coloring*
- *Your Pop Bottle*
- *Water*
- *A white carnation*

### WHAT DO YOU DO?

*1.* Put several drops of red food coloring in your Pop Bottle.

*2.* Fill it full of tap water—leave about 1 inch of space at the top.

*3.* Place the carnation stem in the bottle.

*4.* Wait and see what happens to your white flower.

## WHAT'S GOING ON?

**Y**our white flower becomes a colored flower. Why? Plants are suction machines. They need to have this power to get water up from the ground. In nature, a plant's roots pull water in from the soil. Once inside the roots, the water is pulled up and into all parts of the plant. In this experiment, the red color shows you the water's pathway.

## KEEP GOING!

**Y**ou can make a two-toned carnation by using two pop bottles. Get a grown-up to help you slit the stem of the carnation lengthwise. Place one half of the stem in a bottle with colored water. Place the other half of the stem in a bottle with plain water.

# plant breath

## Watch a Leaf of Lettuce breathe.

## WHAT DO YOU NEED?

- *Your Pop Bottle*
- *Lettuce leaves*
- *Water*
- *A sunny windowsill*

## WHAT DO YOU DO?

*1.* Remove the top of your Pop Bottle and place a few lettuce leaves inside.

*2.* Fill the bottle about three-quarters full of tap water and put the top part back on the bottle.

*3.* Put the bottle near a sunny window and keep an eye on the water. What happens?

## WHAT'S GOING ON?

**A**fter an hour or so, you should start to see little air bubbles forming on the surface of your lettuce leaf. These bubbles are oxygen, the by-product of *photosynthesis*.

Photosynthesis (*photo* = "light," *synthesis* = "to put together") is the process by which plants use water, carbon dioxide, and sunlight to make their own food. As the food is absorbed, the plant's leaves release oxygen into the air. In this experiment, the oxygen is released into the water.

# biome in a bottle

make a miniature ecosystem.

## WHAT DO YOU NEED?

- *Your Pop Bottle*
- *Pebbles*
- *Soil*
- *Seeds (from grass, trees, flowers, vegetables, fruit, or whatever you can easily find)*
- *Water*
- *A sunny windowsill*

## WHAT DO YOU DO?

**1.** Remove the top part from your Pop Bottle.

**2.** Sprinkle 1 inch of pebbles in the bottom of the bottle.

**3.** Add 2 inches of potting soil or topsoil from your yard.

**4.** Run your thumbnail across the center of the soil to make a trench. Sprinkle seeds in the trench, and cover them with soil.

**5.** Water the seeds until you see water collecting in the pebbles.

**6.** Replace the top of the Pop Bottle.

**7.** You've now created a biome.

**8.** Note: You won't need to water the seeds again because the closed Pop Bottle will keep recycling the water through the process of evaporation, condensation, and precipitation. The growing plants need carbon dioxide, however, so you'll need to remove the top of the bottle as the plants begin to grow.

**9.** Put your biome near a sunny window. Your plants should start growing in three or four days.

## BIOME EXPERIMENTS

**Y**ou can imitate the conditions of the world's biomes by changing the amount of sunlight and water your plants receive. A rain forest, for instance, is wet and warm, but the plants there don't get much sunlight. Deserts get a lot of sunlight but not much rain. Grasslands get a lot of sunlight and a fair amount of rain. Under which conditions do your plants do best?

You can also experiment with different types of plants that are ideally suited for certain biomes. Here are some examples:

■ Tropical rain forest: bromeliads, ferns, and common houseplants such as ficus and African violets

- Desert: cacti, aloe vera, and desert succulents

- Grasslands: prairie wildflowers and many kinds of grasses

- Coniferous forests: evergreen seedlings and ferns

- Deciduous forest: ferns, wintergreen, violets, winterberry, strawberries, and blackberries

- Tundra: mosses and lichens

# yeast feast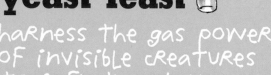

### harness the gas power of invisible creatures to inflate a balloon.

## WHAT DO YOU NEED?

- *A plastic pop bottle*
- *Yeast*
- *Sugar*
- *Warm water*
- *A balloon*

## WHAT DO YOU DO?

*1.* Take the top off the bottle. Sprinkle in ½ teaspoon of dry yeast and 8 teaspoons of sugar.

*2.* Add 1½ cups of warm water.

*3.* Replace the top on the bottle.

**4.** Place the balloon over the mouth of the bottle and wait.

## WHAT'S GOING ON?

**Y**easts eat sugar and produce carbon dioxide gas. As the yeasts gobble up the dissolved sugar in the water, their gas fills the balloon.

# mold garden
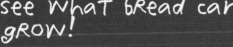
see what bread can grow!

## WHAT DO YOU NEED?

■ *Bread cut into small cubes*
■ *A plate*
■ *Water*
■ *A plastic pop bottle*
■ *A sunny windowsill*

## WHAT DO YOU DO?

**1.** Put the bread cubes on a plate and sprinkle them with a little water.

**2.** Leave the bread cubes out for a couple of hours—even overnight if you can.

*3.* Place the bread cubes into the bottle and tighten the cap.

*4.* Place the bottle on a sunny windowsill and wait for a couple of days.

## WHAT'S GOING ON?

**Y**ou should soon see a bunch of colored fuzz. It could be blue, green, or pink. Most likely you've got a bunch of different molds growing in your garden. When you exposed the bread to air, mold spores fell on the bread and set up shop. With water and bread, molds can reproduce quickly and grow colonies. Don't open the cap or the mold spores could escape into the air, and they might even make you sick. Just observe the mold for as long as you like and then throw the bottle away.

## WANT TO GET HISTORICAL?

**B**ack in 1928, a scientist named Alexander Fleming was working with bacteria. In one of his petri dishes, a bunch of fuzzy mold had begun to grow. The funny thing was that all around the mold, no bacteria were alive. Fleming had discovered a mold that was able to kill bacteria. From this discovery, *penicillin,* an antibiotic that kills harmful bacteria, changed the world of medicine forever. Without penicillin, many people today would die of simple infections.

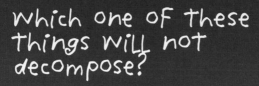 

# to rot or not
## which one of these things will not decompose?

## WHAT DO YOU NEED?

- *4 pop bottles with the tops cut off*
- *Dirt*
- *Fruit slice*
- *Bread slice*
- *Piece of paper*
- *Plastic object*
- *Marker*

## WHAT DO YOU DO?

*1.* Place about 1 inch of dirt in each container.

*2.* Label the containers FRUIT, BREAD, PAPER, and PLASTIC.

*3.* Now put some fruit slices in the fruit bottle, bread in the bread bottle, paper in the paper bottle, and plastic in the plastic bottle.

*4.* Cover each sample with another inch of dirt and place them on a sunny windowsill. Keep the soil moist and wait 4 to 5 weeks.

**5.** Which thing will show no sign of decomposition?

## WHAT'S GOING ON?

**T**he plastic will remain unchanged (aside from getting dirty). How come?

There's an invisible army of creatures in the soil who dedicate their lives to breaking down material and turning it back into soil. These organisms are called *decomposers*. Decomposers can do their jobs on anything that was once living or came from a living thing, but not on man-made materials. Fruit and food come from nature. Paper does, too—it's made from tree pulp. Plastic, on the other hand, can't be broken down into soil.

# worm farm

## do some worm watching.

## WHAT DO YOU NEED?

- *Your Pop Bottle without the top*
- *Sand*
- *Soil*
- *Dead leaves*
- *Bits of potato or onion*
- *Water*
- *Worms*
- *A paper bag*

## WHAT DO YOU DO?

**1.** Make an environment for the worms in your bottle. Start by pouring in about ½ inch of sand. Then add about 2 inches of soil. Continue to alternate sand and soil layers until you have 3 or 4 layers of each. The top layer should be soil. (Don't pack the layers— the sand and soil should be loose.)

**2.** Sprinkle some dead leaves and the bits of potato or onion on top of the final soil layer.

**3.** Spray a little water over the whole thing to make the environment damp.

**4.** Find some worms. After a rain is a good time to look, or under leaves in a shady spot. You're least likely to find worms on a hot sunny day. Worms don't like sunlight or heat.

**5.** Drop the worms into their temporary new home. They will tunnel down into the bottle.

**6.** Cover the top of the Pop Bottle with a paper bag. Worms like dark and damp (but not wet) conditions. Take off the paper bag when you want to worm watch.

**7.** Place the bottle out of direct sunlight and observe what happens over a period of days.

**8.** What happens to the layers of soils you placed in the worm farm?

**9.** After a week or so, return the worms to the outdoors.

## WHAT'S GOING ON?

**G**iven enough time, and enough worms in the bottle, the layers of sand and soil in your Pop Bottle will be completely mixed together.

Worms are essential for life on Earth. They provide a healthy environment for plant life by mixing soil. Their tunnels help bring water and moisture underground. Worms eat all kinds of organic materials and turn them into nutrients for growing things.

# chirping crickets

### how can little crickets make such big noise?

## WHAT DO YOU NEED?

- *A rubber band*
- *Your Pop Bottle without the top*
- *A playing card or index card*

## WHAT DO YOU DO?

*1.* Stretch the rubber band over the bottle opening and under the bottom. Make sure the rubber band is tight.

*2.* Pluck the rubber band with your finger, and with your other hand, touch the rubber band with the edge of the card. You should hear a buzzing sound.

**3.** Experiment and make different sorts of sound. Saw on the rubber band with your card. Pluck the rubber band with your card.

**4.** Now hold a different rubber band between your thumb and index finger. Pluck it with the card. What do you notice about the difference in the volume of sound?

### WHAT'S GOING ON?

**T**he sound of the rubber band is amplified when it is stretched across the bottle opening. The bottle amplifies sound just like the body of a guitar or violin does.

When crickets chirp, they drag their rough upper wing across their lower wing, much as you scrape the rubber band with the card. For crickets, this action produces a vibration that is amplified by the membranes of the wings.

# what is fur for?
## Find out why animals need their fur.

### WHAT DO YOU NEED?
- *Two 2-liter pop bottles*
- *Warm tap water*
- *Hand towel*
- *Rubber bands*
- *Thermometer*

## WHAT DO YOU DO?

*1.* Fill both bottles with warm tap water. The temperature of the water in both bottles should be the same.

*2.* Tighten the caps.

*3.* Wrap the hand towel around one bottle and secure it with a rubber band.

*4.* Put both bottles in the refrigerator for 1 hour.

*5.* Remove the bottles and measure the water temperature.

*6.* Which bottle is cooler?

## WHAT'S GOING ON?

The pop bottle that was wrapped should be warmer (if not, try the experiment again with a thicker towel). The towel created insulation for the bottle, and this helped keep the cold out and the heat in the bottle from escaping. This is what fur is for. An animal's fur coat protects it from cold.

# Light, Sight, Hearing, and Breathing

## big idea

make a bottle magnifier.

### WHAT DO YOU NEED?

- *A plastic pop bottle*
- *Water*
- *Small printed text*

### WHAT DO YOU DO?

**1.** Fill the bottle completely with water.

**2.** Tighten the cap.

**3.** Hold the bottle sideways directly on top of the text. What do you notice?

**4.** Move the bottle slowly away from the small print. You'll see the print flip upside down!

## WHAT'S GOING ON?

**T**he water turns the bottle into a lens, and a lens can do interesting things. When light passes through a lens, an image can twist, bend, curve, and even turn upside down.

# water light
## bend a beam.

## WHAT DO YOU NEED?

- *Plastic pop bottle*
- *Water*
- *A hammer and nail—and a grown-up to help you*
- *An assistant*
- *A dark room with a sink*
- *Flashlight*

## WHAT DO YOU DO?

**1.** Completely fill the bottle with water. Put the cap on tightly.

**2.** Have a grown-up help you hammer a small hole near the bottom of your bottle. (The water won't leak out if the bottle's full and the cap's on tight.)

**3.** Turn the lights off and have your assistant hold the bottle over the sink.

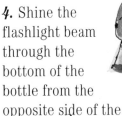

**4.** Shine the flashlight beam through the bottom of the bottle from the opposite side of the hole.

**5.** Have the assistant uncap the top, and watch what happens.

### WHAT'S GOING ON?

**T**he stream of water acts like a hall of mirrors. The light is reflecting back and forth inside the water.

# make a rainbow
### see the colors in sunlight.

### THE FIRST WAY

### WHAT DO YOU NEED?
- *A small mirror*
- *Your Pop Bottle without the top*
- *Water*
- *Sunlight*

## WHAT DO YOU DO?

*1.* Put a small mirror in the bottom of your Pop Bottle.

*2.* Add a small amount of water so that the mirror is submerged.

*3.* Place the bottle in direct sunlight and watch a rainbow appear on a wall.

### THE SECOND WAY

## WHAT DO YOU NEED?

- *A plastic pop bottle*
- *Water*
- *White paper*
- *Sunlight*

## WHAT DO YOU DO?

*1.* Completely fill the bottle with water.

*2.* Take the bottle outside, and find a spot where there is full sunlight.

*3.* Place the paper on the ground, and hold the bottle about 3 to 5 inches above it.

*4.* Move the bottle up and down, or side to side, to focus the sunlight until you see the rainbow.

## WHAT'S GOING ON?

**S**unlight is made up of different-colored lights. We don't see all the colors when sunlight moves through air, but when sunlight hits water, the light bends a little. When this happens, the light fans out and separates into its different colors.

This is how rainbows are formed. After it rains, tiny water particles in the air act just like a bottle full of water. The water particles split the light into different colors, and a rainbow appears in the sky.

# color and heat

## why white clothes keep you cool.

### WHAT DO YOU NEED?

- *Room-temperature black coffee*
- *2 small plastic pop bottles with caps*
- *A thermometer*
- *White paper*
- *A rubber band*
- *Sunshine*

### WHAT DO YOU DO?

*1.* Ask a grown-up to help you get some black coffee.

*2.* Fill each of your pop bottles three-quarters full of cool coffee. Let each of them warm to room temperature.

*3.* Use a thermometer to make sure the temperatures are even in both bottles. If they aren't, wait a while longer and try again.

*4.* Write down the temperatures and tighten the caps.

*5.* Wrap one bottle completely in white paper, securing it with a rubber band.

**6.** Set both bottles in the sun for 1 hour.

**7.** Measure the temperature of both bottles again and write down your results.

**8.** Which bottle is warmer? Which bottle is cooler?

## WHAT'S GOING ON?

**T**he bottle with the white paper is cooler. The color white reflects heat while the color black absorbs heat. This is why light-colored clothes in summer can help you keep cool.

# good vibes
## can you see sound?

## WHAT DO YOU NEED?

■ *Plastic wrap*
■ *Your Pop Bottle without the top*
■ *A rubber band*
■ *Grains of sand or uncooked rice*

## WHAT DO YOU DO?

**1.** Secure a square of plastic wrap around the opening of the Pop Bottle with a rubber band. The plastic should be as tight as a drum.

**2.** Set the bottle on a table and sprinkle a little uncooked rice (or sand) on top of the plastic wrap.

**3.** Stand about 5 inches away from the bottle and talk to it. Sing to it. Hum. Yell. Whisper. Try it from different angles. What happens? Can you make the grains dance?

## WHAT'S GOING ON?

Every sound we make sends a vibration through the air. In this experiment, the grains received the vibrations. This made them bounce, shake, or even dance!

# walkie-talkies

## amplify your voice.

## WHAT DO YOU NEED?

- ■ *The funnel-shaped tops of two plastic pop bottles*
- ■ *A buddy*

## WHAT DO YOU DO?

**1.** Speak into the narrow mouth of the funnel piece, aiming your voice at the listener.

**2.** The listener should try to catch your voice in the wide opening of the funnel, with the narrow mouth pointed toward his or her ear.

*3.* Stand a few feet apart. Chat in a normal voice. Switch roles of listener and speaker. Can you catch what your partner is saying? How far apart can you move and still hear one another?

### WHAT'S GOING ON?

**W**hen you speak into the pop bottle funnel, the sound waves become concentrated. On the listener's end, the wide opening of the funnel acts like a very big ear.

# pop panpipes
## make water music.

### WHAT DO YOU NEED?
- *7 or 8 plastic bottles, all the same size*
- *Water*

### WHAT DO YOU DO?

*1.* Fill the first bottle with about 1 inch of water. Fill the next with 2 inches and the next with 3, and so on until you have filled all the bottles with different amounts.

*2.* Experiment with the sounds each bottle can make. Blow across the tops of the bottles one at a time. Which bottles have a higher sound? Which ones have a lower sound?

*3.* Add and subtract water from your bottles until you get a musical scale you like. (The word *octave* comes from the eight notes in a scale.)

*4.* Try to play a favorite song.

## WHAT'S GOING ON?

When you blow across the top of a bottle, the air vibrates inside the bottle and makes a sound. When you add water, you shorten the air column inside the bottle, and the air vibrates at a higher pitch. When you have less water, the sound is lower.

# trombone

make music with a bottle and a straw.

## WHAT DO YOU NEED?

- *Your Pop Bottle without the top*
- *Water*
- *A straw*

## WHAT DO YOU DO?

*1.* Fill your Pop Bottle with water.

*2.* Put one end of the straw in the water.

*3.* Blow across the top of the straw until you get a sound.

*4.* Once you have the knack, play with the length of the straw that is out of the water.

**5.** What happens to the sound when most of the straw is out of the water? What about when only a little is out of the water?

### WHAT'S GOING ON?

The straw is a column of air. When you blow across the straw, you vibrate the air in the column. The longer the column, the lower the note. The shorter the column, the higher the note.

# bottled breath
## can you see what's in your breath?

### WHAT DO YOU NEED?

- *A deep breath*
- *A plastic pop bottle*
- *A freezer*

### WHAT DO YOU DO?

**1.** Take a deep breath.

**2.** Put the mouth of the empty bottle to your lips, and exhale into the bottle. Seal the cap tightly.

**3.** Put your bottle in the freezer, and wait awhile. What do you see?

## WHAT'S GOING ON?

Your breath is full of water vapor. When you breathed into the bottle and put on the cap, vapor was captured inside. When the bottle was put into the freezer, the vapor returned to water in its liquid state. That's why there's water or ice in the bottom of your bottle.

On a cold day, you can see the water vapor in your breath as a little white cloud. That white cloud is warm water vapor, hitting cold air, and turning from vapor into white liquid droplets.

# lung in a bottle

## how do your lungs pump air in and out?

## WHAT DO YOU NEED?

- ■ *2 balloons*
- ■ *A plastic pop bottle with the bottom cut off*
- ■ *2 rubber bands*

## WHAT DO YOU DO?

**1.** Stuff the large part of a balloon inside the mouth of the bottle. The narrow neck of the balloon should hang outside the bottle.

*2.* Secure the neck of the balloon around the mouth of the bottle with a rubber band.

*3.* This balloon is your lung.

*4.* Cut the neck off the other balloon and fit the large part over the bottom of the bottle. The balloon should cover the bottom of the bottle but not be drum tight. Secure the balloon with a rubber band. (Be sure your bottle is made of sturdy plastic!)

*5.* This balloon is your diaphragm, the tough sheet of muscle that seals off your chest cavity.

*6.* Pull down on the diaphragm balloon. What happens to the lung?

*7.* Push the diaphragm balloon into the bottle. What happens to the lung now?

## WHAT'S GOING ON?

**A**s we inhale, the diaphragm creates space in our chest cavity so air can rush in. As we exhale, the diaphragm compresses the chest cavity, and air is pushed out. If you didn't have this muscle action, you wouldn't be able to breathe.